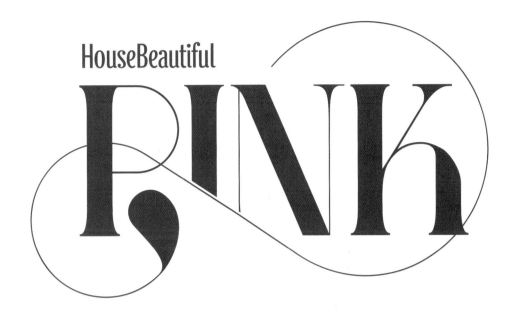

HEARST BOOKS
New York

An Imprint of Sterling Publishing
1166 Avenue of the Americas
New York, NY 10036

ISBN 978-1-61837-185-0

Distributed in Canada by Sterling Publishing
c/o Canadian Manda Group, 664 Annette Street
Toronto, Ontario, Canada M6S 2C8
Distributed in the United Kingdom by GMC Distribution Services
Castle Place, 166 High Street, Lewes, East Sussex, England BN7 1XU
Distributed in Australia by Capricorn Link (Australia) Pty. Ltd.
P.O. Box 704, Windsor, NSW 2756, Australia

For information about custom editions, special sales, and premium
and corporate purchases, please contact Sterling Special Sales
at 800-805-5489 or specialsales@sterlingpublishing.com.

Manufactured in China

2 4 6 8 10 9 7 5 3 1

www.sterlingpublishing.com

HouseBeautiful

PINK

LISA CREGAN

HEARST BOOKS

New York

CONTENTS

INTRODUCTION

Something great happens when you mix a little red pigment into a can of white paint—pink. It elicits an immediate response—it's a passionate color, it can radiate glamour, emit sparks, be traditional or even controversial. And I believe there's a pink for every person, men included. This book will inspire you to find your own shade of pink.

Alongside photos of inspiring rooms, some of America's greatest designers share their secrets for choosing a pink and finding the most complementary colors. As you flip through these pages, designers will also hand you all the tools you need to transform a room with this color—sometimes with a little, sometimes a lot. My own guest bedroom has gone through two pinks over the years, both of which I've loved: Sherwin-Williams' Possibly Pink, a wake up feeling good color, and Ralph Lauren's Santa Rose Suede, a warm cozy color with great texture. Pink has the power to lift your spirit. I'd even go so far as to say it's the color of optimism.

— EDITOR-IN-CHIEF **NEWELL TURNER**

A CLOUD-LIKE PALETTE relaxes the family room of designers Harriet Maxwell Macdonald and Andrew Corrie's Shelter Island beach house.

THAI TOUCH OF PINK

"Color is like jewelry. If you have a basic dress, your jewelry will show in a dramatic way."

—PAT HEALING

IN THE ENTRY

"You know you've got a great color when it hits all your senses. When we talk about atmosphere, we're really talking about feeling and mood. How does nature create atmosphere? Fog. Dappled light."

—SUSAN FERRIER

PALE PINK LAMPSHADES CREATE A WELCOMING GLOW within the dusky gray walls of a Manhattan apartment foyer.

MAUVE-Y WALLS AND A ROBIN'S EGG BLUE COMMODE are surprisingly perfect partners in a New Orleans entry.

DRIFTSCAPE
BENJAMIN MOORE

"My client has a romantic soul. She appreciates the juxtapositions of drastically different things. I began to conceive of the house as a play of textures— of sheen, light, and shadow."

—HAL WILLIAMSON

"Color is the least expensive thing to put in a house. It's a life injection!"

—RUTHIE SOMMERS

A BENCH UPHOLSTERED IN CANDY STRIPE TICKING has old world appeal in an Illinois entry where a botanical mural is painted over chocolate brown walls.

SCONCES LINED IN PINK are covered in scenic wallpaper, a stylish finishing touch in the foyer of a Brooklyn apartment.

"An entrance hall demands drama. It has to be ceremonious."
—TOM SCHEERER

IN THE LIVING ROOM

HOT PINK ACCENTS ARE ALL THAT'S NEEDED to lend an Alabama living room personality.

"It's like hot pink lipstick on a pale face. The throw pillows and the flowers have more oomph because of the contrast with soft-hued neutrals."

—PAIGE SCHNELL

A RASPBERRY LUMBAR PILLOW
resting on a sofa in a Manhattan
living room has big impact in a
sea of blue and silvery white.

"Essentially this is just a blue-and-white apartment, with punctuations of pink to shake things up."

—AMANDA NISBET

"In large spaces hot colors are best used in small doses."

—MARA MILLER

"We went all out for colors that are crisp and cheerful. The room feels vibrant even though the furniture is mostly neutral."

—JESSE CARRIER

A BURST OF FUCHSIA REFRESHES the traditional architecture in a Naples, Florida, living room.

SHADES OF RASPBERRY AND PEACH SOFTEN A SEATING AREA making it plush, but also decidedly informal. A vintage American basketball hoop takes center stage on a rattan scroll table, also vintage. "One thing about Mainers is they're plain folk. You don't want to go up against that too much," Scheerer says.

A PREPPY PINK AND GREEN NEEDLEPOINT CARD TABLE LENDS THE PERFECT TOUCH to the narrative flow here. The room is constructed to feel as though it's been lived in and loved for generations.

"The combination is odd and unexpected but somehow works. I hope it looks improvisational."

—TOM SCHEERER

To enter the living room of this coastal house in Maine is to step back in time. "I was trying to channel the spirit of the grand summer houses of Northeast Harbor. The Rockefellers and Brooke Astor and a lot of the great lady decorators had houses there—Sister Parish decorated Mrs. Astor's house," say Tom Scheerer. **PILLOWS AND WICKER SEAT CUSHIONS IN A SOFT SHADE OF PINK** are part of a purposefully quirky palette that gives the room a layered "house-for-the-generations kind of feeling," the designer says.

ANATOMY OF A LIVING ROOM

DESIGNER
SARA GILBANE

"The painting by Allyson Reynolds above the sofa has some peachy corals, some blush, and rhubarb pinks—one is even a deep scarlet-y pink. They really punch up that wall and take the steam out of any formality."

"Sometimes people say 'oh, but my husband wouldn't like pink'—then it goes up and he loves it!"

"We did the curtains in a beautiful deep color, not magenta, more raspberry. That's when the room started to come to life. The pink gives it a big kick."

"The thing to remember when working with pink is that if you start with a warm pink, stick with that family—don't add a cool shade. Cool pinks have a touch of lavender—warm pinks have more red. Ballet pink, rose pink, they're warm. Peony pink is cool. Cooler pinks would have felt staid in this living room."

◆

"Seafoam and pink is a happy mix and this is the sweetest, happiest family ever. But the Mom isn't a girly girl and neither is her daughter. This room is gender neutral. It's not feminine as much as youthful and fresh."

◆

"I tend to go for happy colors in larger rooms and leave the moody colors for smaller spaces."

◆

"I painted my own living room pink, a rose petal color, a shade lighter than cotton candy—paired with china blue, black, and white—it doesn't take itself too seriously."

bring color and texture to an
otherwise neutral New York
apartment.

"The whole room is neutral. I like to get color in with the accessories—pillows, throws—stuff you can change."

—LILLY BUNN

CONTEMPORARY WORLD INTERIORS

"I learned color discipline by gardening. The foundation of my garden is white, and the only other colors are lavender, soft pink, and green. Once you have a white base you can work out any combination of colors you want."

—PAT HEALING

FRAMED PRINT WITH
...DERTONES is a big jolt
...rnity in a Lake Forest,
...iving room.

"We wanted
the living room
to feel almost
1980s preppy
with matching
pink loveseats.
But it feels
current, too,
because it
has edgy
photography."

—RUTHIE SOMMERS

"This was a delicious opportunity to play around with the fabrics and wallpapers we deal with all day long at Quadrille. The pimento trim pulls everything together."

—JOHN FONDAS

PINK PIPING ON CHAIRS outlines their shapes and contains the pattern, giving this Maine summerhouse's living room crisp appeal.

"The whole room looks like a wrapped gift. It's a vacation house; you want to enjoy yourself. Summer is not a time to be serious."

—JOHN KNOTT

"Think of each fabric as a layer, and play one layer off another. Trust your eye."

—ALESSANDRA BRANCA

OLD-FASHIONED BOTANICAL CHINTZES WITH PINKS FROM FUCHSIA TO PALE feel surprisingly youthful when paired with chartreuse curtains.

"We painted the walls pale blue, added pillows in a variety of textiles, and modernized the lamps with colored shades. It's a more daring spin on traditional."

—SCHUYLER SAMPERTON

IN THE DINING ROOM

"This shade of pink on the walls creates a nice aura. It makes every-one feel good and it makes *me* look good. Pink walls, candlelight— those touches mask a lot of one's sins."

—PETER DUNHAM

A PILLOW-FILLED WINDOW SEAT SET INTO DELICATE PINK WALLS makes for cozy dining in this Los Angeles apartment.

SHIMMERING MAUVE WALLPAPER,
STARK'S COREAN, DOTTED WITH BLUSH
PINK BLOSSOMS evokes a garden at
twilight in a Manhattan dining room.

"We wanted the
dining room to
be a graceful,
elegant jewel
box that glows
in candlelight."

—CHRISTINA MURPHY

"The wallcovering has a lot of luminescence because of the silk stitching on top of the hand-painted paper. Every one of those fish, every flower petal shimmers."

—JOE NAHEM

THE EMBROIDERED WISTERIA AND WATER LILIES in Fromental's Lotus and Carp wallcovering add glittering pink moments and a lot of glamour to the walls of a Greenwich dining room.

ANATOMY OF A DINING ROOM

DESIGNER
LINDSEY CORAL HARPER

"These leather dining chairs are such a beautiful dusty pink—not as vibrant as coral—so wonderfully understated. The shade came straight out of the Oushak carpet. I often pull a subtle color from a rug and play it up in a room. That way you get a broader palette without too many disparate colors."

♦

"I used the same pink that's on the chairs for the valence border and the leading edge of the curtains. So there's pink in the middle of the room, pink on the floor and pink at the wall. It's balanced."

"The prevailing color is a masculine aqua so it's nice to have the contrast of a feminine color for softness."

◆

"The ivory painted table and the pink chairs feel cheerful and young—it doesn't look like your grandparents' dining room!"

◆

"Mirrors double the space here. And they also double the amount of pink!"

◆

"This glass chandelier is completely unexpected and it reflects all the colors in the room."

◆

"I like to put a pattern on the back of dining room chairs. It's nice for your eye to see as you're passing by the room. It gives the chairs more life."

◆

"Pink is a great color for master bedrooms and bathrooms, too, because people look good in blush colors and those are the rooms where makeup is applied and hair is arranged. And in a dining room, pink makes everyone at a dinner party look and feel fantastic."

IN THE FAMILY ROOM

LUSH TEALS AND SILVERS MIX WITH FUCHSIA to brighten this family room even on the gloomiest Manhattan day.

"My client was very particular about wanting strong fuchsia and turquoise. But too much would have been aggressive. We needed white and gray to ground it."

—FAWN GALLI

> "Bits of pink are tamed by browns, pale blues, and creams."
>
> **—JONATHAN BERGER**

THE PILLOWS' HAPPY SHADE OF ROSE was pulled from the art in a Brooklyn family room.

MOOD BOARD

Designer Lauren Nelson creates a family room with just a hint of fuchsia.

"I love hot colors but you don't have to go overboard with them to have a lot of impact. I'd use fuchsia only for the throw pillows in this family room to bring in a just a bit of pink rather than doing a whole chair in it. Bold color that's balanced, that's what I love."

———◆◆———

"I would paint walls Pratt and Lambert's Winter's Gate—my favorite gray. Some grays have green undertones, some are too blue or purple—this paint color is a neutral middle ground, perfect to use with pink."

———◆◆———

"I'd add touches of organic texture—a table with a concrete top and a blackened steel base, a rug with off-white tones and a chunky weave. Those things wouldn't intrude on the color palette and they add presence. I would also bring in some brass because I think fuchsia and brass look great together—but only brushed brass, never polished."

———◆◆———

"Dark stained walnut is my absolute favorite wood for floors or bookshelves; it has gorgeous grain and looks handsome with pink because it has no red undertones."

———◆◆———

"I like neutral sheers at the windows to get the most natural light possible."

———◆◆———

"Just a little bit of fuchsia would go a long way here and everything else should be calm for serenity."

———

1. Cherry blossom branches
2. Dara Rug in cream from Restoration Hardware
3. Votives from Z Gallerie
4. Footed Table by John Dickinson through Sunderland
5. Plumwich's Pierre fabric in Chocolate Brown
6. Lisa Fine Textiles' Aswan in Passion
7. Granada Pendant Lamp from Laviva Home
8. Paused Rope Lamp from Anthropologie

"I positively adore all iterations of pink and gray—soft muted pink with gray, bright fuchsia with gray. Pink and gray is never wrong except when you use Pepto-Bismol baby pink—you know that traditional nursery pink? No matter what you combine it with, it looks too preppy!"

—LAUREN NELSON

IN THE KITCHEN

PRIMROSE AND TROPICAL GREEN TAKE THE ENERGY LEVEL UP in a Malibu kitchen where the palette reflects the energetic young family who lives here.

"From the beginning, we knew we were dealing with clients who were very color-expressive."

—TODD NICKEY

GARDEN PINKS AND SKY BLUES combine with trellised walls to mimic the interest of the landscape outside this Connecticut kitchen's windows.

"I thought those chairs really needed some fabric to give the white-white kitchen a burst of color."

—ALLISON CACCOMA

HITS OF PINK take this Boston kitchen from strictly utilitarian to warmly welcoming.

"I wanted the kitchen to be cohesive, not monotonus."

—NINA FARMER

THE SOFT COLORS IN THE WATER LILIES AT THE WINDOW and the movement in the veining of Calacatta Gold marble tiles banish blandness in this white-on-white Gibbsboro, New Jersey, kitchen.

"White is a classic color for a kitchen, and I thought it was appropriate for this classic, Colonial-style house. And we picked up the gold in the marble tile with brass hardware and brass light fixtures."

—CAITLIN WILSON

AT WORK

A DESK CHAIR IN A CHEERFUL STRIPE
has the energy needed to jazz up
gray cabinets in an Alabama kitchen.

"Pink is
the owner's
favorite color.
She's blonde,
and she wears it
all the time."

—DOUG DAVIS

A BLOWN-UP ANTIQUE MAP WITH SWATHS
OF TERRACOTTA AND PEACH is endlessly
enthralling for the eight-year-old boy
who does his homework here.

"I love a room
where you can
create a happy
mess and it just
makes it feel more
comfortable."

—DANIEL SACHS

IN THE BEDROOM

"Colors look richer when they're paired with neutrals. I tend to go for taupe and gray-beige, something that looks like it might be found on a beach. With a gray tone you can add any color."

—BETSY BURNHAM

GRAY AND PEACH for a Los Angeles teenage girl's bedroom is both sophisticated and youthful, a palette she can grow into.

"It's all about balance. That big old comfortable bed and lots of painted paneling—they balance out the pink chairs."

—SUZANNE RHEINSTEIN

"The master bedroom is soft, subtle, and refined. It invites light, air, and the silvery reflections from the water out the windows."

—MARSHALL WATSON

A COOL COLOR PALETTE PROVIDES SANCTUARY from the Naples, Florida, sun, while a raspberry-skirted table pulls the eye out to the water view.

A SPIRITED PARROT PRINT DUVET LIFTS THE MOOD of a dark and serious wall color in this Vermont bedroom.

"Even though we live here full-time, we tried to design our house with the feeling of a country house that we escape to."

—DEIRDRE HEEKIN

SOFT BLUE WALLPAPER WITH DELICATE TOUCHES OF PALE PINK and a vibrant, vintage suzani bedspread bring Hollywood glamour to this Los Angeles master bedroom.

"Pink jazzes up a room. Pink is whimsical and fun and such a happy color."

—RUTHIE SOMMERS

"This isn't a gag-me pink. It's utterly soft, and we used it in blocks with lots of white. The iron bed helps to control it, and so do the brown and pink bed linens."

—GARY MCBOURNIE

A SOFA COVERED IN THE SOFTEST PINK IMAGINABLE—Groundworks' Academy Weave in Light Pink—is a soothing spot for an afternoon nap in this Palm Beach master bedroom.

EN PLEIN AIR

LARGE BLUSH THROW PILLOWS BRING SUMMER CHEER and invite visitors to enjoy the water view from this Maine porch.

"It's a sixth sense for when to slow down, pull back. I don't like things that are overstyled."

—TOM SCHEERER

"Simplicity is really the height of elegance, and style is all about confidence."

—BARBARA BARRY

A FEW PASTEL STRIPED PILLOWS AND A PINK HYDRANGEA serve to heighten the appeal of the terrace outside a house in Corona del Mar.

ON A WATCH HILL, RHODE ISLAND, PORCH, pink provides the spark of happiness atop cushions that harmonize with the soft grays of the house's shingles.

"A two-color scheme can be great, but there has to be some relief, or it comes across as too pat and makes everything seem stiff."

—TOM SCHEERER

"I used this pink in my first studio apartment in New York. There was something about the combination of this color and the afternoon light pouring through the floor-to-ceiling windows that was so calming. You might think a pink apartment would scream 'girly girl,' but the gray undertones make it more sophisticated and grown-up."

—ASHLEY WHITTAKER

Farrow & Ball
Estate Eggshell Pink Ground

Farrow & Ball
Estate Emulsion Pink Ground

ON THE WALL

"This is a fleshy pink, which makes it more sophisticated and versatile. With the right lighting, it really glows, and that's such a warm and welcoming way to be introduced to someone's home. Pair it with some strong, slightly masculine pieces to add visual weight. An antiqued brass mirror and a dark wood console would do the trick."

—MONA ROSS BERMAN

Apricot Ice
Valspar

"I tend to lean toward lighter tones in a small space, so it doesn't cave in. This has a freshness that feels open and breathable. I see it in a small, enclosed porch with hand-blocked linen in white, blue, and lavender. The sun is setting and it's time to curl up with a glass of white wine and a good book. I want to be there now!"

—REBECCA TIER SOSKIN

"I know, I know, you're thinking no man wants to sleep in a pink bedroom. But there's nothing baby or bubblegum about this pink. You could say it's the ultimate aphrodisiac, because there's not a woman alive who wouldn't feel pretty surrounded by this color. That's incentive enough for any man to go along with it, don't you think?"

—SHEA SOUCIE

Fine Paints of Europe
Camellia Pink

Victorian Lace
Benjamin Moore

"In an introspective room where you go to think and read, flesh tones work very well because they have an engulfing, comforting quality. This is a pale face-powder shade, with a sensuality about it that would also suit a bedroom. It makes everybody look wonderful and creates a sense of intimacy."

—VICENTE WOLF

Demure
Sherwin-Williams

"Guys, don't be afraid. You may think this is pink, but it has a touch of burgundy that makes it way more sophisticated. Coupled with flannel grays or camel, it will make you feel all dressed up."

—GIDEON MENDELSON

"Lusterware has those iridescent pink and copper tones and looks so pretty inside a dining room cabinet. This would accentuate the pink and give the room a warm glow, and that makes everyone feel more attractive. Watch out—pink is one of those colors that intensifies on the wall, so err on the side of lighter."

—TODD RICHESIN

Benjamin Moore
Pink Swirl

Paris Pink
Valspar

"I like using pink in an unexpected place like a kitchen or an entryway. It's flattering and familiar, soft and warm like skin. We think of pink as an old lady color, but it can be very young if used the right way—with touches of cobalt blue, red, orange, or green. If everything is too pastel-y, it looks like a nursery."

—JACKIE TERRELL

"There's a softness to this cream, with a touch of red, that attracts me. That bit of warmth makes it more uplifting. It's like a blossom in spring. I would do it in a bedroom with olive, navy, or eggplant. It's gentle and clean and optimistic— a fresh way of being Zen."

—BRETT BELDOCK

Pantone
Delicacy

Pink Bliss
Benjamin Moore

"We used this barely-there pink in a home office that opened to a small courtyard garden. The pale petal color played up the greenery outside, making it feel more like a garden room than a work environment. It was soft and cushiony, as if we had replaced the walls with a billowing cloud."

—AMY KEHOE

"I love pink. It makes me feel warm and fuzzy. I just want to slip on a ruffly boudoir jacket and lean back into the pillows and eat chocolate. This pink is very soft and feminine, but it's not sticky. Pair it with white or metallic surfaces to make it ethereal and inviting."

—PHOEBE HOWARD

Sherwin-Williams
White Dogwood

DESIGNER KRISTA EWART uses punches of happy pink to enliven her sister's Balboa Island, California, beach house.

2

MORE PINK

"This office feels like a fabulous compartment on the Orient Express. You're not sure where you're going, but you're very happy while you're getting there."

—T. KELLER DONOVAN

IN A PALM BEACH APARTMENT, a pink and white palette helps the office double as a guest room.

IN THE ENTRY

"I've been working on a hacienda for a client that's all about Morocco meets Mexico meets Africa, and I was inspired by all those bright colors."

—KATHRYN M. IRELAND

A DAYBED WITH PINK AND GOLD PILLOWS IS AN INVITING PLACE to perch in an Ojai, California, farmhouse.

"Something happens when you put a gold-leaf console against a humble ticking stripe wall. That traditional shape becomes fresh and young. That's what I love."

—ALESSANDRA BRANCA

"I call this coral sofa the 'love love seat'—it's so small two people will sit there only if they're in love."

—MIMI MCMAKIN

A WELCOMING POP OF COLOR on a settee adds zest to a Palm Beach foyer.

AN INTRICATE 19TH-CENTURY
CAUCASIAN CARPET SETS OFF
a settee with hints of pink.

"You start
with the rug.
That was the
best advice
David Hicks
ever gave me."

—PETER DUNHAM

IN THE LIVING ROOM

FUCHSIA AND CHERRY RED ARE SURPRISINGLY ATTRACTIVE PARTNERS in a corner of a Manhattan living room.

FUCHSIA AND CHERRY RED ARE SURPRISINGLY ATTRACTIVE PARTNERS in a corner of a Manhattan living room.

"The sofa is bright and fresh. And there's something utilitarian about it, like an army-navy store."

—MILES REDD

THE ROSY HUE OF PINK-STRIPED
SLIPCOVERS CONTRASTS with
apple green walls for maximum
drama in this Locust Valley,
New York, living room.

"This house isn't at all bashful."

—JEFFREY BILHUBER

THE INTENSITY OF FUCHSIA IS TEMPERED by chocolate brown and porridge-y beige in the living room of a Brooklyn townhouse.

"This client went for pink right away. It's an all-girl household, and she wanted to celebrate that fact."

—JONATHAN BERGER

SPIRITED COLOR ON BERGÈRES BRINGS A LIGHTHEARTED ATTITUDE to this small apartment. But the navy trim under the nailheads "gives weight to the chairs and makes them feel important," Whittaker says.

A SWATH OF PINK IN AN ABSTRACT PRINT over a desk at one end of the living room jibes with the color of the chairs on the other side. When entertaining, the desk is used as a dining table or a buffet.

"Touches of gray—on the slipper chair and settee and in the rug under the desk—add neutrality and keep the place from looking so girly-girly."

—ASHLEY WHITTAKER

A bright chair and pillows signal that this Manhattan apartment belongs to a young woman in her 30s with a sense of style. Even though the living room is only 300 square feet, Ashley Whittaker says, **"WHEN IT COMES TO COLOR, 'GO BIG OR GO HOME.'** You have to trust yourself."

POLKA DOTS, PRINTS, AND ALL SHADES OF PINK AND GREEN mix together in a happy jumble in a Balboa Island, California, beach house.

"I use a lot of pink but my style isn't all that girly. It's not all ruffly, bows, and rosebuds. It's fresh, playful, and modern, and that doesn't offend the husbands!"

—KRISTA EWART

MOOD BOARD

Designer Alexandra Kaehler creates strong presence in a master suite

"In Chicago, where I live, winters are dreary so I like to bring bright pink into bedrooms to make a cold gray morning feel more cheerful. But when you have a room with strong pops of raspberry like this, you need to use a blush pink elsewhere in the room—to repeat pink but in different iterations adds interest without being match-y."

♦

"I would use lamps made of something like quartz because an organic element creates romance, a more dressy feel than a ceramic lamp. And an end table with graphic brass legs adds nice modern geometry to a floral chintz. I think of brass in the same way I think of pink, they both warm up a space."

"I would paint the walls a charcoal gray, Farrow & Ball's Down Pipe, and use black and white bedding topped with a four-foot-long bolster covered in this Schumacher Elizabeth floral chintz. It's a really strong fabric and would be all you need for bold contrast against neutrals."

♦

"I saw a photo of a bedroom Mary McDonald did that really inspired me. She used navy and white as the main base colors and then brought in fuchsia pillows and pink accents to enliven the palette."

♦

"Pink peonies are my absolute favorite for bedrooms—they're so much more relaxed than roses which, to me, connote a bit more formality and structure."

---

1. Suwan Sisal in Sharkskin from Schumacher

2. Elizabeth in Grey/Rouge from Schumacher

3. Valhalla Chic Lamp from Times Two Design

4. Rosy-Cheeked Coupe from BHLDN

5. Shut the Door, Have a Seat from Soicher Marin

6. George Table from Oly

7. Pink peonies

"Pink can be very sophisticated if you create a lot of contrast. There's a harsh graphic masculine quality to the black-and-white I've chosen for this bedroom but when it's up against pink it's elevated. I'm always looking for balance—pink is the great mediator."

—ALEXANDRA KAEHLER

> "If this house has a mandate, it's to not take itself too seriously."
>
> —ALESSANDRA BRANCA

POPS OF ROSE AND RED on a seductive banquette that fills a bay window in a Chicago living room make it irresistibly intimate and warm.

ANATOMY OF A LIVING ROOM

DESIGNER
FAWN GALLI

"I go into people's closets to get a sense of their style. This client had Pucci prints, fashion-forward clothes and colorful accessories, and she was very particular about wanting strong fuchsia and turquoise accents throughout her house. We brought in this fabulous stained-glass-style rug that has every color of the rainbow and it really pulled the living room together."

———◆◆———

"The walls needed depth and personality. We used a Fine Paints of Europe lacquer—a light green with blue in it—which reflects light."

"Knowing how to stop at just the right moment makes all the difference. We did the chairs in a pink cheetah print, used Missoni fabric at the windows, and piped the sofa cushions in hot pink—that's where we stopped and said 'No more pink!'"

♦ ♦

"The sofa is a cocoa color—a great foil for hot pink. The pink piping outlines the shape but it also pulls pink to that side of the room for balance."

♦ ♦

"Once we decided to use a large-scale pattern on the draperies and the rug we knew we needed a smaller scale for the chairs. They are 1950s chairs but I think the fabric makes them feel current."

♦ ♦

"The kind of pinks you see in India are the ones I like best—saris with an antique feeling and such. There's a soulfulness to those shades. But I also like dreamy, American girly pink—you can't beat a 1960s ladies' pink suit."

"Color makes me happy. And that was the direction with this apartment—to make a happy family home."

—MILES REDD

JEWEL TONES LEND
POWERFUL CHARACTER
to a Manhattan living
room where pink is
so strong it feels
almost masculine.

IN THE DINING ROOM

STRIPED CURTAINS COMPLEMENT THE FLORAL WALLPAPER and pull a delicate shade of pink out of the Oriental rug in this Los Angeles dining room.

"It's is a little bit granny— but granny chic. The room is small so we wanted to make it a pretty jewel box with the wallpaper as the focal point."

—SCHUYLER SAMPERTON

SIMPLY HANGING A CHEERFUL
FABRIC ON THE WALL instantly
transformed this Pasadena
office from bland to brilliant.

"I have a textile
addiction!"

—LINDSAY REID

IN THE FAMILY ROOM

A CARNATION PINK AND TANGERINE PALETTE in a Connecticut family's sunroom evokes an old-fashioned screened-in porch.

"The palette is a great way to suggest sun on a gloomy day."

—STEVEN GAMBREL

THE CORAL AND BLACK PALETTE in this Chicago family room is family friendly and sophisticated at the same time.

"These clients are a young couple with two boys and a terrific sense of humor. This room is the whole family's big media room and so we used a very forgiving tree-of-life pattern on the sectional."

—ALESSANDRA BRANCA

"I wanted to give this new house a strong, creative personality and a sense of patina and history."
—JEFFREY BILHUBER

HAPPINESS IS CREATED when a pink sofa is paired with a floral carpet in a Bedford, New York, family room.

ANATOMY OF A FAMILY ROOM

DESIGNER
BETSY BURNHAM

"Pink makes an unexpected statement in this family room, but not a feminine one. The pink is balanced here by really really powerful neutrals."

◆ ◆

"This is a Tudor home that's kind of dark so we were trying to lighten it up. We were originally going to use the pink Quadrille chinoiserie only for pillows but then we thought, 'Why don't we use it on the sofas?' Because the fabric is only two colors, it feels bright and modern."

"The husband really wanted to be able to put his feet up so we added a vinyl rattlesnake-pattern ottoman on top of a faux zebra rug. We used tons and tons of grays and browns like that to surround the pink with colors and rich textures that would keep it from being too sweet."

◆ ◆

"The pillows are vintage suzanis. I didn't worry about matching."

◆ ◆

"Fuchsia's not my style, and I stayed away from it. I think an intense shade of pink makes a room too contemporary. My palette tends toward classic Dorothy Draper or Lanvin pink, rooted in history."

◆ ◆

"I didn't use much black here. Black and pink is too strong and Art Deco for me. I'm subtler than that."

◆ ◆

"For walls, I love Farrow & Ball's Pink Ground, a peachy, cameo pink that's super flattering, sophisticated and never looks juvenile."

IN THE KITCHEN

A LIVELY BACKSPLASH is the focal point of a Manhattan kitchen.

"We found this embroidered fabric with just the right handcrafted, cheerful touch (Lee Jofa's Laueretta). So we laminated it between two sheets of glass and used it for the backsplash."

—ADAM ROLSTON

PINK AND SKY BLUE IS A VERY ANIMATED PALETTE, so the charcoal gray island became crucial to keeping things grounded.

"Varying the colors in a room makes the space feel bigger, believe it or not."

—ADAM ROLSTON

IN THE BEDROOM

"The silver threads in the blue-green wallcovering in the teenage daughter's bedroom have so much feminine glamour."

—LEE ANN THORNTON

A COZY READING SPOT AND A WORK AREA WITH POPS OF PINK are nestled into niches.

"Cheerful, joyful. You just can't walk in without thinking, 'this feels good.'"

—LEE ANN THORNTON

BLUSH PILLOWS ADD FEMININE BALANCE to a headboard covered in a dhurrie rug. "This is done to the nines," Nye says. "I recently contemplated doing my bedroom ceiling with raffia wallpaper, but my friends all told me to 'Stop decorating!'"

"I HAVE AN EERO SAARINEN SIDE TABLE NEXT TO A FRANCES ELKINS DRESSING MIRROR. You need some contrast to rooms," Nye says, "When everything is of the same great pedigree, rooms look like museums. I didn't want my bedroom to look like Babe Paley's."

"The mix gives good tension to my bedroom. I do have a lot of girlie but I have masculine pieces too."

—JOE NYE

PINK IS A SOFT SURPRISE IN JOE NYE'S LOS ANGELES BEDROOM. He loaded the room with furnishings, some of them big-scale pieces like a buffet by Frances Elkins and a 19th-century lantern from Hollyhock. "You practically have to walk sideways to get around. But I live alone, so 'sensible' doesn't have to prevail."

"It feels so
good—not
dark—just very
very relaxed."
—PHILIP COZZI

PEONY PINK SILK PILLOWS, MADE FROM A 1920S CHINESE CURTAIN, SPRAWL on a glittery yellow damask coverlet to enliven chalky green painted walls in a Provincetown summer cottage.

"You wake up and feel incredibly rested. This bedroom is like a dream machine."

—KRISTIN HEIN

"I wanted
this room to
be breezy and
light-spirited."

—TOM SCHEERER

A LUSH PEACH-PAISLEY TEXTILE
drapes a four-poster bed
to create coziness and a
sense of architecture in a
Pennsylvania bedroom.

A LAVISHLY PATTERNED WINDOW SHADE AND A FRENCH SETTEE introduce pink into this Los Angeles bedroom in a sophisticated way.

"We used a copy of a Louis XVI settee and put a serious raspberry silk damask on it. I wanted it girly without being silly."

—JOE NYE

THE PATTERN OF THE BLACK AND FUCHSIA PILLOWS ON THE BED echoes the butterfly wings in the wallpaper. "The home was designed to feel like a whimsical, wintry forest," Galli says, "Call it surrealism grounded in nature. Or nature with a twist."

A SHADE TRIMMED IN HOT PINK BALL FRINGE dresses up a custom sconce. "It's a 21st-century version of an old romanticism—like the vivid interiors in Sofia Coppola's *Marie Antoinette*, which definitely influenced this place," Galli says.

"The daughter's room has a dreamlike, enchanted feeling, with butterflies flying around."

—FAWN GALLI

Fuchsia upholstery on a Lucite chair adds bold presence to a young girl's Manhattan bedroom. **"IN SMALL ROOMS, LUCITE FURNITURE AND PALE CARPETS MAKE THINGS MORE AIRY,"** says Fawn Galli, "Unless you're in a Chelsea gallery, I think ebonized floors and that whole dark, minimal Christian Liaigre look is over. It just doesn't give enough to a room. I prefer Baroque and Rococo-style curves and Barbara Barry furniture, which feels French 1940s yet American at the same time."

IN THE BATH

"I stacked three towel bars like a ladder— that makes the towels so much more approachable and humorous."

—JEFFREY BILHUBER

AN ARRAY OF LADYLIKE HAND TOWELS IN PASTEL COLORS in a Bedford, New York, powder room contrasts with the rough-cut marble sink basin.

SALMON-HUED STONE lends this new bathroom in the Hamptons an ancient-European feel.

"Elegance is refinement. It's when you can't pinpoint when a room was done. It could have been years ago or yesterday."

—NOEL JEFFREY

EN PLEIN AIR

"You mustn't overthink it. I see it in my head very quickly and I seldom change my concept."

—PODGE BUNE

TRIM IS CACTUS FLOWER
BENJAMIN MOORE

A SWINGING DAYBED CASUALLY STREWN WITH **PINK AND PURPLE** patterned pillows on a Palm Beach porch is a charming place to perch.

"The cushion is simply covered with a tablecloth, and I threw some random pillows on it. I don't care if it all matches. If it's perfect, where's the fun?"

—LIZA PULITZER CALHOUN

THERE'S A HEALTHY DOSE OF PINK in an al fresco dining room where a jasmine vine climbs the wall between mirrored trellises outside a Palm Beach maisonette.

"We gave the walled courtyard the same attention to detail as we gave the house's interior."

—MIMI MCMAKIN

PRETTY IN PINK AND GREEN, the table's palette is nearly synonymous with its location—Palm Beach.

"What's more romantic than eating under the stars?"

—MIMI MCMAKIN

"Pink may be the navy blue of India, but coral is the beige of Hawaii. This is a real late-1940s, early-1950s coral, deep and rich. It's Debra Paget wearing a sarong in *Bird of Paradise*. It's sex on the beach . . . with great lighting. I throw this color on ceilings— that's a Billy Haines trick. He knew it would make everybody look great."

—JARRETT HEDBORG

Benjamin Moore
Bird of Paradise

Sherwin-Williams
In the Pink

ON THE WALL

"Here in Florida, I have the most wonderful porch that has been painted pink for 30 years. It's the pink of strawberry ice cream cones and climbing roses and the blush on our cheeks after a long luxurious day at the beach."

—MIMI MCMAKIN

Benjamin Moore
Coral Gables

"This is warm and inviting. It reminds me of the glow of the sun. When I look at it, I feel as if I'm on an island in the Caribbean, which is where I find most of my inspiration. I'd layer it with natural linens and white trim."

—ELSA SOYARS

"I did a black, white, and gray kitchen in Palm Beach, but it was leaving us a bit chilly. So we painted the ceiling hot pink, and the insides of the cabinets a lighter version of the same shade. The color is a surprise and a delight. It made the ceiling soar and gave the space a whole new energy."

—PATRICK KILLIAN

"This really does look like the inside of a mouse's ear. It's a good clear pink that has very little blue in it, so it doesn't turn cold. Pink is a color with a lot of animation. There's almost a fey quality to it. You could bring in apple green or bachelor-button blue or stay with white. I once did a living room in pink and white and beige, like a conch shell."

—LIBBY CAMERON

"This pink reminds me of opals and pearls, Jean Harlow and silk charmeuse, 'New Dawn' roses and a baby's rosy cheeks. Who wouldn't want a perpetual glow like that? When it comes to decorating, it's perfect with black and white and everything in between. And real men do like pink—they just might not admit it at first!"

—CHARLOTTE MOSS

"Pink all by itself can be perceived as feminine, but what you pair it with makes all the difference. Think of a man in a black suit with a pink shirt and tie, or plopping a pink sofa into a listless beige room. Pink is suddenly daring and electric. The right shade of pink can energize any space."

—KELLY WEARSTLER

"The ceiling is the most overlooked and underused opportunity in decorating. I usually opt for an ethereal shade like this pink—the color of a raspberry mousse, luscious and delectable. It brings your eye up and automatically raises the ceiling height."

—JAMIE DRAKE

Colonial Rose
Fine Paints of Europe

"I had a client, a very elegant man in his seventies, who requested a pink bedroom. He was a widower, and it reminded him of his wife. I think men like pink more than they're willing to admit. I have a pink living room with zebra-upholstered doors. Men tend to like warm colors. This pink has a happy carnation quality in bright sunlight and gets more glowy and dusty at night."

—MILES REDD

Pink Harmony
Benjamin Moore

"A south-facing room is more flexible when it comes to choosing colors. And it doesn't necessarily have warm light, especially in the Northern Hemisphere, so you don't have to stick with green or blue. I tend to like colors that are warmer to begin with, so I'd go with pink. Then you get all those beautiful transitions from pink to peach to golden yellow during the day."

—STEPHEN SHUBEL

"What makes a dark-haired woman look good is a glow of color. This soft, sensual peach has the romance of candlelight and the warmth of cashmere. If a woman paints her bedroom this color, a man might think it's too feminine until he's in it. But then he would feel enveloped and embraced, warm, cozy, taken care of—all those things people like to feel."

—SUSAN ZISES GREEN

Benjamin Moore
Perky Peach

Gentle Butterfly
Benjamin Moore

"This apartment has a very happy vibe, just like the woman who lives here. We both love pink, and I found this romantic, grown-up pale peony pink for her. Subtle, yet strong enough not to wash out in all the natural light. It's cheerful in the morning but not too bright at night. It doesn't scream at you if you're reading in bed or trying to sleep."

—BROOKE GOMEZ

A YOUNG GIRL'S MANHATTAN BEDROOM—designed by Kemble Interiors—is drenched in pink starting with walls painted Benjamin Moore's Rosetone.

3

A PROFUSION OF PINK,

"Pink is a wonderful color. I did blush pink walls and the pattern on the sofa is sort of like pink cherry blossoms."

—CARLETON VARNEY

IN THE ENTRY

TERRACOTTA TRIM and a Swedish bench create painterly beauty in this Maine farmhouse entry.

"The clients were unafraid of color. That was one of the most fun aspects of the project."

—KARI MCCABE

VIBRANT WALLS SET OFF by white balusters and a mint green handrail come as a complete surprise when the door opens to this Maine entry.

RED EARTH
FARROW & BALL

"The colors are idiosyncratic, personal, and much more vibrant than the standard white or gray."

—KARI MCCABE

IN THE LIVING ROOM

"This place is ladylike, but it's also strong, like an atomic explosion—a big bomb of pattern."

—T. KELLER DONOVAN

SALMON PEACH
BENJAMIN MOORE

"The pink in
the living room
just felt au cou-
rant—like the
right pink for
the moment."

—JAMIE DRAKE

TREATED WITH A LIGHT
BRONZE GLAZE TO GIVE
THEM PEARLESCENCE, THE
PINK WALLS in this
Manhattan living
room steal the show.

"Salmon pink is happy and familiar. Everyone's skin looks amazing with it. It's neither too feminine nor too masculine with the energy to hold a room whether day or night."

—ROB SOUTHERN

TO CAPTURE A COUNTRY COTTAGE LOOK in an East Hampton living room, the same Brunschwig & Fils pink chintz is used on all the upholstered furniture.

"We wanted it fun, fresh and funky, with lots of humor and even a teeny-tiny bit campy."

—JOE NYE

BRIGHT RASPBERRY IS ALL THAT'S NEEDED TO ADD YOUTHFUL MODERNITY to a Los Angeles apartment where the furniture shapes are traditional.

"I like a mix of Indian, African, Islamic, Chinese, Danish, French, Italian, and American. Even the diluted pink on the walls has this Indian or Mediterranean quality."

—PETER DUNHAM

ATMOSPHERIC PINK WALLS play up exotic fabrics and accessories for global sophistication in this Los Angeles apartment.

SAFEPAINT WHITE
WITH 10% BARN RED

SHADES OF PINK THAT DELIBERATELY DO NOT MATCH the Cole & Son's Cow Parsley wallpaper give this Maine living room a breezy, devil-may-care attitude.

"For the wife, color meant a warm and welcoming house, where family and friends would be comfortable."

—KARI MCCABE

"Pink here is really faded red. It's pink with a past."

—ELLEN O'NEILL

THE SOFTNESS OF WORN WEATHERED PINK completely relaxes the mood in this Bridgehampton, New York, beach house.

"When I was a child, I used to go with my mother to a shop on Park Avenue. I would see her trying on these beautiful clothes, and I was always so fascinated by the fabrics. It was the beginning of a lifelong love."

—ALEX PAPACHRISTIDIS

A FEARLESS PALETTE OF HOT PINK, CHERRY RED, AND EGGPLANT in Papachristidis' Manhattan living room transforms an ordinary Manhattan apartment into an exotic haven from city life.

THE UNBRIDLED USE OF SOFT CORAL PINK is balanced by the rugged textures of wicker and dark, stained wood in this Pasadena living room.

"I was inspired by the relaxed charm of houses in places like Portofino, Ravello, and St. Tropez. I wanted to embrace this house's unpretentious atmosphere with warm colors that would conjure up free-spirited comfort."

—LINDSAY REID

IN THE DINING ROOM

"I often take one color and delve into it in different ways. A supersaturated color pops so vibrantly."

—HEATHER CHRISTO

MASS QUANTITIES OF DEEP CORAL translate into luxury in a Seattle dining room.

GUESTS ENTER THIS MIAMI HOME'S DEEP RASPBERRY DINING ROOM through its blush pink living room as if hopping from one square to another in a paint-chip color book.

"I like to find colors that are sort of odd together. They set up a kind of vibration."

—GENE MEYER

"I think of my rooms as conservative but elegant, and that's one of the reasons I like to use related chintzes—subtle combinations make rooms blend together."

—JUSTINE CUSHING

A DECADES-OLD PINK COTTON FABRIC COVERS TALL DINING CHAIRS, originally made to go with the flowery curtains in this Hamptons cottage.

ROMANTIC COLORS AND EXOTIC PATTERNS ARE GROUNDED by a strong English table in this Newport Beach, California, dining room.

"We mixed Raj glamour with Uzbekistan, Persia, Sri Lanka—and a little Moroccan hookah den."

—KATIE MAINE

> "Pink was our main state-ment, taming it with browns, pale blues, and creams."
>
> —JONATHAN BERGER

HOT MAGENTA CHAIRS DRAW THE EYE down the middle of a long and narrow Brooklyn living room.

CHAIRS UPHOLSTERED IN A FLAME STITCH VELVET raise the pink level to high in this exuberant Lake Forest, Illinois, dining room.

"This dining room feels like a petit four or a piece of candy. The pink lamps just made us happy and we lacquered the walls robin's egg blue because, well, why not?"

—RUTHIE SOMMERS

ANATOMY OF A DINING ROOM

DESIGNER
KELEE KATILLAC

"The walls are upholstered with silk because silk reflects light much the same way a rose quartz crystal does. And worldwide, rose quartz is associated with affection and love. It's a wonderful color to replicate in a dining room."

◆ ◆

"Curtains are in the same pink fabric as walls. I wanted to see what would happen if we treated the curtains as ball gowns—with hand pleats, double top stitching, and triple lining—against more tailored walls."

"This Vervain silk looks different at different times of day. On a gray day it has more of a blue tint, on a sunny day more peach."

♦ ♦

"I added taupe to the room to make it comfortable for both ladies and gentlemen. And the heavy rustic look of the table contrasts with the reflective nature of the pink walls. Below the chair rail I applied a linen fabric with a cut velvet pattern. Chair rails were originally invented in the 18th century to protect against chairs bumping against the walls; that's why this pattern has a Georgian quality to it."

♦ ♦

"The cotton slipcover on the wing chair relaxes the room. It's done the way it would have been done in the service wing of an old English country house."

♦ ♦

"Some of the great painters of the Fauvist era in France in the 1920s would use a little bit of pink in every painting because it amplifies other colors like blue. I think it's the same in decorating."

IN THE BEDROOM

SATURATED COLOR PACKS
A PUNCH in Kathryn Ireland's Ojai, California, guest room.

SATURATED COLOR PACKS A PUNCH in Kathryn Ireland's Ojai, California, guest room.

"I love these bright pinks and green, and the juxtaposition of a William & Mary bed with that oversize photo looks so modern."

—KATHRYN M. IRELAND

"I have a kind
of fearlessness,
along with
a sense of play.
I don't take
myself
too seriously."

—AMANDA NISBET

A DOUBLE HEADBOARD PULLS
TOGETHER A BRAVE COLOR PALETTE
and unites twin beds in this
Manhattan bedroom.

IN A RAMBLING SUMMER COTTAGE IN EAST HAMPTON, the designer embraced his client's "romantic, old-fashioned side" in the master bedroom. A blush floral fabric and pillows with fuchsia monograms create the ultimate romantic bed.

A LADYLIKE ANTIQUE DAYBED creates a cozy reading spot. "The goal was to make multigenerational, intimate rooms that would feel as good to a child as to a great-grandfather."

"The client loves fabrics with a flower-on-vine motif, and the whole room casts the most beautiful soft-pink glow. It's enchanting."

—ROB SOUTHERN

The entire master bedroom is swathed in delicate pink. Designer Rob Southern used the same fabric for the walls, curtains, seating, bed corona, and headboard. "We've done what people have done in Palm Beach and other resort communities forever, which is to **COVER EVERYTHING IN ONE FABRIC**—it's a great way to unify disparate things," he says.

ANATOMY OF A BEDROOM

DESIGNER
LIBBY CAMERON

"I used pink layer-upon-layer in this master bedroom. This Osborne & Little wallpaper is a delicate blush pink so we had to go for a deeper coral for the headboard or the room would have looked far too sweet. And because of the large-scale pattern of the wallpaper, every other pattern had to be a smaller scale for harmony."

"The owner already had the bedding in these pretty sorbet colors and we added even more peach. I actually love the combination of pink with peach."

"If we hadn't had the head-board's border gathered, it wouldn't have had nearly enough weight against the busy wallpaper."

◆ ◆

"If you have pale pink walls you need to use stronger shades of pink throughout the room so you're not competing with the walls. Vice-versa too!"

◆ ◆

"I'm a big fan of combining pink and red like this, but you have to be careful. You know how some pinks can feel blue and some can feel yellow? The same goes for reds. So you shouldn't combine a yellow-tinted pink with a red that has blue undertones. You have to be consistent, or it doesn't work."

◆ ◆

"Even just a bit of pink has clout. Nancy Lancaster had a room in her house in Oxfordshire that had a wonderful pink chair I often think about. That one chair evoked a pink sense in the entire room."

"Pink and orange isn't a combination you see much of. Pink and green would have been the easy way out, but it would have taken things in a preppy direction. This house is more subversive than that!"

—MONA ROSS BERMAN

ELECTRIC COLORS BRING ZEST AND ZING to a master bedroom in a 1960s-inspired beach house in Strathmere, New Jersey.

IN A PRETEEN DAUGHTER'S CAPE COD
BEDROOM, WAVY FUCHSIA STRIPES BURST
from the quilt and make the whole
room feel spirited and youthful.

"When you're twelve, you need a sassy room. This daughter's credo was 'the brighter, the better.' We started with a happy green base and added pink, orange, and aqua."

—ANNIE SELKE

THE CORNERS IN THIS LAKE FOREST, ILLINOIS, BEDROOM are outlined in pink tape to play up its architectural angles.

"I don't think florals should go in and out of style, so I just keep using them and wait for things to circle back around."

—RUTHIE SOMMERS

TO ENSURE THE GUEST ROOM IS COLORFUL but not cacophonous, it's completely enveloped in the same pattern—Cowtan & Tout's Amelie.

"It looks like someone moved in and thought, 'Oh this wall-paper's kitschy, let's keep it.'"

—RUTHIE SOMMERS

MOOD BOARD

Designer Patrick Mele uses a riot of pink in the bedroom.

"I'm drawn to the kind of pinks you see in Italy, terracotta orange-y pinks—a little sexy, mature, and sensual. Francois Nars makeup really inspires me. And the sunset pinks the painter J.M.W. Turner used."

◆ ◆ ◆

"Walls in this bedroom would be upholstered in pink silk, floors in Farrow & Ball Calluna. Windows and trim in Farrow & Ball Pelt and the doors Farrow & Ball Brassica in full gloss. The ceiling would be 22k gold leaf. It's a fantasy room!"

◆ ◆ ◆

"Pink light bulbs would be fantastic here. Keith McNally uses them in all his restaurants. Everyone looks dewy, young, and alive."

"I think Olatz sheets trimmed in purple would be such a regal touch in this bedroom."

◆ ◆ ◆

"Clarence House's Velours Uni in Rubris is the most beautiful raspberry velvet you've ever seen. It would make a wonderful headboard."

◆ ◆ ◆

"Pink and gold or brass is a combination I adore so I would place a gilt Chinoisserie mirror over a fireplace—very Anne Getty—and Rigaud candles on the mantel, they come in pink wax!"

◆ ◆ ◆

"As a final touch I'd use an apricot Noguchi round lantern in the middle of this bedroom ceiling, all wonderfully warm, glow-y and pinkish."

---

1. Standard Gilded Orchids by Tommy Mitchell

2. Schumacher's Babe's Tweed

3. Schumacher's Classic Corduroy in Fuchsia

4. The Tizio Lamp

5. India Silk by Elitis

6. Painting by Jenny Andrews-Anderson

7. Still Table by Rodolfo Dordoni

"This bedroom is an exotic maximalism pink fantasy. A little **Ottoman Empire**, a little Venice—sexy, sensual, exotic— a spicy jewel-toned fantasy retreat."

—DESIGNER PATRICK MELE

THE WALLS IN AN ELABORATELY
FEMININE DRESSING ROOM on
Long Island are covered in
fabric—Travers' Hydrangea
& Rose.

"I wanted to do
a pretty, fancy
lady's dressing
room as a part
of the master
suite. I said,
'Let's do it in
this wonderful
old fashioned
chintz.'"

—MARKHAM ROBERTS

PEONY PINK FABRIC PROVIDES CONTINUITY in a young girl's Manhattan bedroom where curtains, walls, and desk are all covered in Les Indiennes' Duchesse.

"There's something to comfort and ease, to having a room where you can put a book down and it blends into the landscape."

—DANIEL SACHS

IN THE BATH

"I see this as very modern even if the components aren't; they reflect the way I live my life today."

—JEFFREY BILHUBER

A VINTAGE SINK AND A PINK STRIPE SKIRTED CHAIR feel spun from the past in Bilhuber's newly freshened Locust Valley, New York, bathroom.

"For me, the
test is how do
you feel when
you open the
door? If you
don't feel happi-
ness, something's
not right."

—ROYCE PINKWATER

A PHOTO UNDER GLASS CREATES A WINDOW
where there is none in this Manhattan
master bathroom.

IT'S NOT JUST THE COLOR PINK THAT FEELS '30s AUTHENTIC in this young girl's bathroom. "I wanted the vanities to have the flavor of 1930s cabinetry, with glass pulls and a scalloped skirt," Stuart says, "The counter is marble with a honed finish, to make it feel as if it has been there for some time. The sink is a classic oval, and I chose faucets with cross handles because they're reminiscent of the original fixtures."

BLACK OUTLINES THE ENTIRE ROOM AND MAKES PINK STAND OUT. "The black acts as a border," says the designer. "It accentuates both the architectural elements and the tile itself. Black is like an exclamation point."

"Our mandate when we took on this restoration was to create the impression that the house had barely changed since it was built in the thirties."

—MADELINE STUART

The bold use of tilework in this Beverly Hills bathroom may look original to the 1930s but every square foot is all new. **EACH CALAMINE PINK TILE IS SLIGHTLY DIFFERENT, CREATING A WATERCOLOR EFFECT.** "We worked with a wonderful company, Mission Tile West, that can re-create the translucency of the 1930s glazes," says Madeline Stuart.

HOT HOT HOT PINK WALLS upholstered in Amanda Nisbet Design Textiles' Positano is somewhat tempered by black in a Manhattan powder room.

"Before I became a designer, I had a job working with gemstones. Such luminosity, such brilliant hues! It transformed my eye."

—AMANDA NISBET

A RIOT OF PINK is created when a Brooklyn bathroom's walls are covered in China Seas' Lysette.

"'Exuberantly feminine, yet resolutely chic,' that became our motto."

—JONATHAN BERGER

"I have a room with red velvet furniture and I put hot pink on the walls, breaking all the rules I was taught in school. Other rooms are purple, pea green, and Mykonos blue, creating this wonderful pathway of color through a dark interior. I see these colors in my head, and it's like having a mystical experience. I have to incorporate them into my world."

—HUNT SLONEM

Ellen Kennon Full Spectrum Paints
Hot Pink!

ON THE WALL

Ralph Lauren Paint
Racer Pink

"Everywhere you go on the island of Capri you see masses of climbing bougainvillea vines clinging to white-washed houses. The hot pink flowers are papery and delicate, but somehow the color feels almost like neon in the bright sun. It's very alive and invigorating. Use it as an accent to give any room a lift."

—JONATHAN ROSEN

Lime Wash Pink Ginger
Sydney Harbor Paints

"The whole city of Jaipur, India, is painted pink. It's an exuberant color, optimistic and positive. Jaipur pink reminds us that we're all alive and everything is possible. I like this type of paint, because it has a chalky layer underneath that blooms through and gives it a patina. Try it with saffron and orange."

—WINDSOR SMITH

"Leave the other walls white and put the accent on the wall that gets the most sun. It will bounce back into the room and suffuse it with color. This is an amazing pink with a tiny bit of lavender in it. It will warm up the whole room. And if you're stressed, pink is known to be tranquilizing. Prisons paint the cells of the most dangerous inmates in pink!"

—BENJAMIN NORIEGA-ORTIZ

Benjamin Moore
Pretty Pink

Priscilla

Sydney Harbour Paints

"This is a pulsating hot pink. I would do it with white trim and ebonized black floors, a white Moroccan rug, shades of indigo on the furniture. Or maybe saffron and tangerine. You walk in and feel incredibly happy."

—MARCY MASTERSON

Exuberant Pink

Sherwin-Williams

"India is all about sensory overload. More is more. Every destination is a psychedelic blur of color— market stalls filled with heavy clusters of red bananas and green mangoes, temples with Hindu deities garlanded in orange marigolds, and bright silk saris in this vivid pink, crimson, magenta, blue, or violet, mirrored and embroidered with golden threads."

—KATHRYN M. IRELAND

"I bought an antique games table and knew I would never find chairs to match. Since it was going into a playroom I thought, 'Why not be playful?' So I went to Crate & Barrel and picked up four modern Windsor chairs and painted them bright pink. Fabulous next to the dark wood."

—SCOTT SANDERS

Benjamin Moore

Glamour Pink
Benjamin Moore

"I love designing powder rooms because it's an opportunity to do something you wouldn't do in a larger space. For one client, we painted the entire room rosy pink, gold-leafed every inch of the moldings, and did a custom mosaic glass floor in pink and gold. It was over the top. It glowed. And everyone looked fabulous in the mirror!"

—JAY JEFFERS

"I can't think of a better room for a brunette than Harry's Bar in Florence, with begonia pink walls and dark wainscoting. The tablecloths and napkins are the same pink with a hint of blue in it, which makes it a tad cooler. Rich colors are really flattering to brunettes, while blondes just fade away. But stay away from sweet, or anything that looks like it would be appropriate for Easter."

—JARRETT HEDBORG

Milano Red
Benjamin Moore

"We were looking for an updated West Coast version of the famous Diana Vreeland red and found this saturated pink. In gloss, it has even more depth. It's not for the faint-of-heart, and it works best in a transitional space—definitely not the most restful tone for a bedroom! The intensity is a commitment, but it can really lift the light, accent art, and point up woodwork. We paired it with white moldings and a glossy black door."

—KRISTEN BUCKINGHAM

Old World
Benjamin Moore

"This lush coral makes you feel as if you're walking into a conch shell. It's happy and bright. You might not be able to live with this amount of color in a living room, but in a small, featureless entry with lots of doorways, a dramatic paint color is the best way to create a sense of place."

—VICTORIA NEALE

Sedona Pink
Ralph Lauren Paint

"In a white bedroom with navy blue fabrics, I painted the ceiling hot pink. When you're lying in bed, there's nothing like a reflective wash of pink to make your entire body look warm and sexy, head to toe. It's a great seduction trick, kind of like wearing lingerie under a trench coat."

—MARY MCDONALD

Benjamin Moore
True Pink

Checkerberry

Glidden

"It's important when you use a bold color like this that you make sure it has enough depth. I wanted some gray and also some brown undertones in this pink. Colors that have no depth are oddly florescent."

—SUZANNE KASLER

PHOTOGRAPY CREDITS

INDEX